For Ruth, Johnny and

Anna with all my love.

B.C.

HODDER CHILDREN'S BOOKS
First published in Great Britain in 2023 by Hodder and Stoughton
First published in paperback in 2024

1 3 5 7 9 10 8 6 4 2

A CIP catalogue record for this book is available from the British Library.

HB ISBN 978 1 44495 312 1
PB ISBN 978 1 44495 313 8

Printed and bound in China

FSC www.fsc.org MIX Paper from responsible sources FSC® C104740

Hodder Children's Books
An imprint of Hachette Children's Group
Part of Hodder and Stoughton
Carmelite House, 50 Victoria Embankment, London, EC4Y 0DZ

An Hachette UK Company
www.hachette.co.uk
www.hachettechildrens.co.uk

THE MAGIC OF ME!

Hodder
Children's
Books

Today I can be **ANYTHING**,

Anything at all!

My head is full of great big dreams

Although I'm only small.

Today I'll be **CREATIVE**

And paint and stick and draw.

I'll make a **magic** castle,

Then open up the door . . .

Today I will be **CURIOUS** –
The world is for exploring!
Shhh! I'll tiptoe oh-so-carefully
Past creatures who lie snoring.

Today I will be **BRAVE**,

Whatever comes my way.

I'll find the **strength** inside me

To chase my fears away.

Today I will be **NOISY**,
As **LOUD** as I can be!
I'll **CRASH** and **BANG** and sing a song.
Come on, join in with me!

Today I will be **BUSY**.
I'll cook a tasty feast –
Enough to feed an army
Of hungry little beasts!

Today I'll be

INVENTIVE

And build

fantastic

things,

With bucket loads
of bits and bobs,
Some cogs
and bouncy springs.

Today I will be **CARING**

For creatures young and old,

From crocodiles with crooked tails

To a lion with a cold.

Today I'll be **ADVENTUROUS**
And zoom up to the stars!
I'll loop-the-loop round Jupiter,
Then stop for tea on Mars.

Today I will be **QUIET**,
Taking time to wonder why
The world is always spinning
And the sun shines in the sky.

Today has been AMAZING –
As fun as fun can be!
ANYTHING can happen
When you let your dreams run free.

But what will I be tomorrow?

I'll have to wait and see.

There's one thing that I know for sure . . .

. . . it's **MAGIC** being

ME!